This book belongs to:

_____

A catalogue record for this book is available from the British Library

Published by Ladybird Books Ltd
80 Strand London WC2R 0RL
A Penguin Company

2 4 6 8 10 9 7 5 3 1
© LADYBIRD BOOKS LTD MMVIII
LADYBIRD and the device of a Ladybird are trademarks of Ladybird Books Ltd

ISBN: 978-1-84646-820-9

Printed in China

My best book about...
Farms

Written by Stella Maidment
Illustrated by Katie Saunders

Farms are important places.
Can you find a farm in this picture?

Some farmers keep cows to give us milk. Which two cows are different from the others?

A tanker comes to take the milk away. Can you help this tanker to find the farm?

Some farmers keep chickens.
Can you find three eggs?

Some farmers keep sheep and lambs.
Tell this story about Mary and her lamb.

Does it remind you of a nursery rhyme?

The farmer's dogs are very clever.
They show the animals where to go.

How many sheep are in the pen?

Some farms grow fields of crops, like wheat or barley.

What is happening in these pictures?

③

④

Some farms have all sorts of different animals. Can you say what all these animals are?

Farmers grow fruit and vegetables too. How many creatures are hiding in this strawberry bed?

Most of the things we eat or drink started life on a farm. Can you match the food to the place it came from?

Farmers are very busy people.
Where is each of these farmers going?

If you were a farmer, what would you have on your farm?

Which jobs would you like the best?